PICTURE THIS!
Shakespeare

William Shakespeare's

A Midsummer Night's Dream

EDITED BY
Philip Page and Marilyn Pettit

ILLUSTRATED BY
Philip Page

BARRON'S

First edition for the United States, its territories and dependencies,
the Philippine Republic, and Canada published in 2005 by
Barron's Educational Series, Inc.

All inquiries should be addressed to:
Barron's Educational Series, Inc.
250 Wireless Boulevard
Hauppauge, New York 11788
www.barronseduc.com

International Standard Book No.: 0-7641-3142-7

Library of Congress Catalog Card No.: 2004110785

Printed in China
9 8 7 6 5 4 3 2 1

Contents

About the play

A Midsummer Night's Dream is a comedy. Shakespeare's comedies follow a formula. The rules mean that however many bad things happen, and however many obstacles there are to make people unhappy, the audience knows that they will be overcome in the end. His comedies usually end with a wedding and a party.

This comedy has young lovers forbidden to marry; the threat of death; mysterious happenings in sinister woods; spells that cause trouble and chaos; mad chases; a man turning into an ass; and a very funny play within a play.

Read on. As you do, note the comic effects, the problems that occur, and the way they are resolved.

Literary terms

alliteration The repetition of one or more beginning sounds, usually consonants, in a group of words.

comedy A form of literature in which characters are faced with moderate difficulties, but they overcome them and the story ends happily.

hyperbole Language that greatly overstates or exaggerates for rhetorical or comic effect.

irony Term indicating that the way something appears differs from reality, either in meaning, situation, or action. It is ironic when there is a difference between what is said and what is meant (verbal irony), what a character believes about a situation and what is reality, or what is intended by a character's actions and what is the actual outcome (dramatic irony).

metaphor A figure of speech that compares unlike objects without using connecting terms such as *like* or *as*.

oxymoron A statement that combines two terms usually seen as opposites. The effect created seems to be a contradiction, but is true. Some examples are *deafening silence, jumbo shrimp*.

personification A figure of speech in which objects or animals are given human qualities.

simile A figurative comparison using the words *like* or *as*. Some examples are *pretty as a picture, cunning like a fox*.

soliloquy A speech given in a drama, when characters speak their thoughts aloud while alone, thereby communicating their thoughts, mental state, intentions, and motives to the audience.

tragedy A form of literature in which the hero is destroyed by a character flaw and a set of forces that cause the hero considerable suffering.

Many examples of these terms have been pointed out for you throughout this book. Pay attention and you may find even more!

Cast of characters

Theseus
Duke of Athens.

Hippolyta
Queen of the Amazons
who marries Theseus.

Hermia
A fiery young
lady.

Lysander
Hermia's loyal
boyfriend.

Demetrius
A young man who
loves Hermia.

Helena
A young lady in
love with
Demetrius.

Egeus
Hermia's very angry
father.

Philostrate
Theseus' servant, in charge
of the entertainment!

Oberon   **Titania**

King and Queen of the Fairies.

Puck

Oberon's mischievous servant. Also known as **Robin Goodfellow**.

A group of tradesmen who are planning to entertain the Duke with their play:

Peter Quince   **Nick Bottom**   **Francis Flute**

A carpenter.   A weaver.   A bellows-mender.

Tom Snout   **Snug**   **Robin Starveling**

A tinker.   A joiner.   A tailor.

Act 1 Scene 1	Theseus and Hippolyta look forward to their wedding. Theseus wants all of Athens to be happy.

Now, fair Hippolyta, **our nuptial hour** draws on apace. Four happy days! How slow this old moon wanes!

Four days will quickly steep themselves in night; four nights will quickly dream away the time: and then the moon shall behold the night of our **solemnities**.

Go, Philostrate, stir up the Athenian youth to merriments.

Hippolyta, I won thy love doing thee injuries; but I will wed thee with pomp, with triumph and **revelling**.

our nuptial hour – the time of our wedding
solemnities – festive ceremonies; wedding ceremony
revelling – partying

<table>
<tr><td>

**Act 1
Scene 1**

</td><td>

Egeus is angry. His daughter refuses to marry the man of his choice. She faces a horrible future!

</td></tr>
</table>

Egeus: Happy be Theseus, our renownèd Duke!

Theseus: Thanks, Egeus. What's the news with thee?

Egeus: Full of **vexation** come I, with complaint   anger
Against my daughter Hermia.
Stand forth, Demetrius!
This man hath my consent to marry her.
Stand forth, Lysander!
This man hath bewitched my child.
Lysander, thou hast given her rhymes,
And interchanged love-tokens:
Thou hast by moonlight at her window sung.
With cunning hast thou **filched** my daughter's heart,   stolen
Turned her obedience (which is due to me)
To stubborn harshness.
And she will not consent to marry Demetrius.
I beg the ancient privilege of Athens,   I'd like to use an old law of Athens
As she is mine, I may dispose of her
Either to this gentleman or to her death.

Theseus: What say you, Hermia?
To you your father should be as a god.
Demetrius is a worthy gentleman.

Hermia: So is Lysander.

Theseus: In himself he is;
But, **wanting your father's voice**,   without your father's support
The other must be held the worthier.

Hermia: I would my father looked but with my eyes.

Theseus: Rather your eyes must with his judgment look.

Hermia: I beseech your grace that I may know
The worst that may befall me
If I refuse to wed Demetrius.

Theseus: Either to die, or to **abjure**   give up
Forever the society of men.
Examine whether (if you yield not to your father's choice)
you can endure the **livery of a nun**.   clothes worn by a nun
Happy is the rose **distilled**   picked to make perfume
Than that which, withering on the virgin thorn,
Grows, lives, and dies in single blessedness.

Hermia: So will I grow, so live, so die, my lord,
Ere I will yield my virgin patent up   before I'll marry
Unto his lordship whose unwished yoke
My soul consents not to give sovereignty.

Theseus: Take time to pause, and by the next new moon –
The **sealing day** betwixt my love and me   wedding
Either prepare to die or else to wed Demetrius,
Or to **protest** for single life.   prepare; vow

Literary terms

"prepare to die or else
to wed" is an example of
hyperbole.

Think about it

What evidence is there that
Theseus is fair?

Do you think Hermia is brave
or foolish?

Relent, sweet Hermia; and Lysander, **yield thy crazèd title to my certain right**.

You have her father's love, Demetrius – let me have Hermia's.

True, he hath my love.

She is mine, and all my right of her **I do estate unto** Demetrius.

I am, my lord, as well derived as he, my love is more than his; and I am beloved of Hermia.

Demetrius made love to Helena, and she dotes upon this **spotted** and inconstant man.

I have heard so much.

Demetrius, come, and Egeus; You shall go with me.

Hermia, fit your fancies to your father's will, or else the law of Athens yields you up to death, or to a vow of single life.

Yield ... right – give up what is mine
I do estate unto – I give to

spotted – morally stained, wicked

4

My love? Why is your cheek so pale? The course of true love never did run smooth.

O hell! – to choose love by another's eyes.

I have a widow aunt, she hath no child. From Athens is her house seven leagues. She respects me as her only son.

There may I marry thee, and the sharp Athenian law cannot pursue us.

If thou lovest me, then **steal forth** thy father's house tomorrow night; and in the wood, there will I **stay** for thee.

I swear to thee by Cupid's strongest bow, in that same place tomorrow will I meet with thee.

steal forth – sneak out of
stay – wait

5

Here comes Helena.

Fair Helena! Whither away?

Call you me "fair"? Demetrius loves **your fair**.

I frown upon him, yet he loves me still.

O, teach me how you look, and with what art you sway the motion of Demetrius' heart.

O that your frowns would teach my smiles such skill!

I give him curses, yet he gives me love.

O that my prayers could such affection move!

The more I hate, the more he follows me.

The more I love, the more he hateth me.

your fair – your fairness, beauty

6

Take comfort. He no more shall see my face. Lysander and myself will fly this place.

Tomorrow night through Athens gates have we devised to steal.

And in the wood shall meet, and from Athens turn away our eyes.

Pray for us; and good luck grant thee Demetrius.

Adieu!

Through Athens I am thought as fair as she. But what of that? Demetrius thinks not so. Love looks not with the eyes, but with the mind. Ere Demetrius looked on Hermia's eyne. He hailed down oaths that he was only mine.

I will go tell him of fair Hermia's flight. Then to the wood will he, tomorrow night, pursue her.

Think about it

What does Helena hope to achieve by telling Demetrius?

<table>
<tr><td>**Act 1
Scene 2**</td><td>A group of tradesmen meet to plan the play they want to perform for the Duke's wedding.</td></tr>
</table>

Quince: Is all our company here?

Bottom: You were best to call them generally, man by man, according to the **scrip**.

script

Quince: Here is the scroll of every man's name which is thought fit, through all Athens, to play in our **interlude** before the Duke and the Duchess, on his wedding day at night.

an entertainment that comes between other events

Bottom: First, good Peter Quince, say what the play treats on; then read the names of the actors.

Quince: Our play is "The most **lamentable** comedy, and most cruel death of **Pyramus and Thisbe**."

sad

Pyramus and Thisbe – the story of Pyramus and Thisbe, a story very much like that of *Romeo and Juliet*.

Bottom: A very good piece of work and a merry. Call forth your actors by the scroll.

Quince: Answer as I call you. Nick Bottom, the weaver?

Bottom: Ready! Name what part I am for, and proceed.

Quince: You are set down for Pyramus.

Bottom: What is Pyramus? A lover or a tyrant?

Quince: A lover, that kills himself for love.

Bottom: That will ask some tears in the performing of it. If I do it, let the audience look to their eyes! **I will move storms. Yet my chief humor is for** a tyrant. Name the rest of the players.

I'll make them cry so much! But I'd really like to act as ...

Quince: Francis Flute, the bellows-mender?

Flute: Here, Peter Quince.

Quince: Flute, you must take Thisbe.

Flute: What is Thisbe? A wandering knight?

Quince: It is the lady that Pyramus must love.

Flute: Let me not play a woman – I have a beard coming.

Quince: You shall play it in a mask. You may speak as **small** as you will.

shrill; high-pitched

Bottom: I may hide my face. Let me play Thisbe too. I'll speak in a **monstrous little** voice: "Thisne, Thisne!" – "Pyramus, my lover dear!"

extremely small

Literary terms

"monstrous little" is an example of an *oxymoron*.

Quince: No, no; you must play Pyramus; and Flute, you Thisbe.

Bottom: Well, proceed.

Quince: Robin Starveling, the tailor?

Starveling: Here, Peter Quince.

Quince: You must play Thisbe's mother. Tom Snout, the tinker?

Snout: Here, Peter Quince.

Quince: You, Pyramus' father; myself, Thisbe's father; Snug, the joiner, the lion's part.

Literary terms

"Snug, the joiner" is an example of *play on words*.

Snug: Have you the lion's part written? If it be, give it me; for I am slow of study.

Quince: It is nothing but roaring.

Bottom: Let me play the lion too. I will roar.

Quince: You would fright the Duchess and the ladies and that were enough to hang us all.

Bottom: I will roar as gently as any sucking dove.

Quince: You can play no part but Pyramus. Pyramus is a sweet-faced man; a most lovely, gentleman-like man.

Literary terms

"as gently as any sucking dove" is an example of a *simile*.

Bottom: Well, I will undertake it. What beard were I best to play it in?

Quince: What you will.

Bottom: Either your straw-color beard, your orange-tawny beard, your purple-in-grain beard, or your French-crown-color beard, your perfect yellow.

Quince: Here are your parts; **con** them by tomorrow night; and meet me in the palace wood by moonlight. There will we rehearse, for if we meet in the city we shall be dogged with company, and our devices known.

learn

Bottom: Take pains, be perfect.

Quince: At the Duke's oak we meet.

Think about it

Do you think anyone would want to copy their idea?

Why does Quince's worry about this make us laugh?

Puck meets a fairy in the wood. He tells her about the quarrels the Fairy King and Queen are having. Oberon and Titania meet and begin to argue.

anon – soon
passing fell and wrath – in a really angry mood
square – quarrel

Ill met by moonlight, proud Titania!

What, jealous Oberon? Fairy, **skip hence. I have forsworn his bed and company**.

Tarry! Am I not thy lord?

Then I must be thy lady.

skip hence – leave
I have . . . company – I don't want anything to do with him
Tarry! – Wait!

Hippolyta, an Amazon warrior

Titania: Why art thou here, but that **the Amazon**,
Your mistress and your love
To Theseus must be wedded – and you come
To give their bed joy and prosperity?

Oberon: How canst thou thus, for shame, Titania,
Knowing I know thy love for Theseus?

Titania: These are the forgeries of jealousy;
And never since the **middle summer's spring**   beginning of midsummer
Met we, but with thy brawls
Thou hast disturbed our sport.
The winds, in revenge, have sucked up from the sea
Contagious fogs; the moon, pale in her anger,
Washes all the air that rheumatic diseases do abound.

Oberon: Do you amend it then! It lies in you.
I do but beg a little changeling boy
To be my **henchman**.   page, squire

Titania: The fairy land buys not the child of me.
I will not part with him.

Oberon: How long within this wood intend you stay?

Titania: Perchance till after Theseus' wedding day.
If you will dance and see our moonlight revels,
Go with us.

Oberon: Give me that boy, and I will go with thee.

Titania: Not for thy fairy kingdom! Fairies, away.
We shall **chide downright** if I longer stay.   definitely quarrel
                      [*Exit Titania and her fairies*]

Oberon: Thou shalt not from this grove
Till I torment thee for this injury.
Puck, come hither. Thou rememb'rest
That time I saw Cupid?
He loosed his **love-shaft** from his bow.   arrow
It fell upon a little western flower,
Before milk-white; now purple with love's wound.
Fetch me that flower;
The **juice** of it, on sleeping eyelids laid   nectar from the flower
Will make or man or woman **madly dote**   fall madly in love with
Upon the next live creature that it sees.

Puck: I'll put a girdle round about the earth
In forty minutes! [*Exit Puck*]

Oberon: I'll watch Titania when she is asleep,
And drop the liquor of it in her eyes.
The next thing she, waking, looks upon
She shall pursue it with the soul of love.
And ere I take this charm from off her sight
I'll make her render up her page to me.

Literary terms

"fell upon a little western flower,…Fetch me that flower;" is an example of *alliteration*.

Think about it

Is Oberon acting fairly?

Is he just jealous or is he trying to restore order?

Demetrius comes into the wood to find Hermia. He is angry because Helena has followed him.

Who comes here? I am invisible, and I will overhear their conference.

Where is Lysander and fair Hermia? Thou told'st me they were stol'n unto this wood.

Get thee gone, and follow me no more.

You draw me, **you hard-hearted adamant**.

I do not, nor I cannot love you.

Even for that do I love you the more. Give me leave to follow you.

I am sick when I do look on thee.

I am sick when I look not on you.

you hard-hearted – your heart is as hard as stone
adamant – like a magnet

You do impeach your modesty to commit yourself into the hands of one that loves you not; to trust the opportunity of night and a desert place with your virginity.

It is not night when I do see your face. You are all the world.

I'll run from thee and hide me in the **brakes**, and leave thee to the mercy of wild beasts.

Let me go.

If thou follow me, I shall do thee **mischief** in the wood.

I'll follow thee, and make a heaven of hell, to die upon the hand I love so well.

You do … commit – You're not very sensible, putting …
brakes – bushes
mischief – harm

Literary terms

"make a heaven of hell" is an example of an *oxymoron*.

While Titania sleeps, Oberon squeezes the love juice into her eyes. His plan for revenge is under way!

Come, a fairy song. Sing me now asleep. Then let me rest.

You spotted snakes with double tongue,
Thorny hedgehogs, be not seen.
Newts and blind-worms, do no wrong,
Come not near our Fairy Queen.
Weaving spiders, come not here;
Hence, you long-legged spinners, hence!
Beetles black, approach not near;
Worm nor snail, do no offence.

Away! Now all is well.

What thou seest when thou dost wake, do it for thy true love take. Wake when some vile thing is near!

While Lysander and Hermia sleep, Puck mistakenly squeezes juice into Lysander's eyes. Meanwhile, Helena is left alone. She wakes Lysander, who immediately falls in love with her!

Lysander: I have forgot our way.
We'll rest us, Hermia, if you think it good,
And tarry for the comfort of the day.

Hermia: Find you out a bed,
For I upon this bank will rest my head.

Lysander: One turf shall serve as pillow for us both.

Hermia: Nay, good Lysander; for my sake, my dear,
Lie further off yet; do not lie so near.

Lysander: I mean that my heart unto yours is knit,
So that but one heart we can make of it.
Then by your side no bed-room me deny,
For lying so, Hermia, I do not lie.

Hermia: Lysander riddles very prettily.
But, gentle friend, for love and courtesy
Lie further off, in human modesty.
Such separation as may well be said
Becomes a virtuous bachelor and a maid.
Good night.

Lysander: Here is my bed; sleep give thee all his rest.
[They sleep. Puck enters.]

Puck: Who is here?
Weeds of Athens he doth wear:
This is he my master said
Despisèd the Athenian maid.
And here the maiden, sleeping sound,
On the dank and dirty ground.
Churl, upon thy eyes I throw
All the power this charm doth **owe**.
[Exit Puck. Enter Demetrius and Helena, running.]

Literary terms

"One turf shall serve as pillow" is an example of a *metaphor*.

Literary terms

"sleeping sound," "dank and dirty," and "Churl… charm" are all examples of *alliteration*.

You miserable boy
own; possess

20

Helena: Stay, sweet Demetrius!

Demetrius: Do not haunt me thus.

Helena: I am out of breath in this chase!
But who is here? Lysander on the ground?
Dead, or asleep? I see no blood, no wound.
Lysander, if you live, good sir, awake!

Lysander: [*Waking*] And run through fire I will for thy
sweet sake!
Where is Demetrius? O how fit a word
Is that vile name to perish on my sword!

Helena: Do not say so, Lysander,
though he love your Hermia
Hermia still loves you; be content.

Lysander: Content with Hermia? No.
Not Hermia, but Helena I love.

Helena: When at your hands did I deserve this scorn?
You do me wrong.
O that a lady, of one man refused,
Should of another therefore be abused!

[*Exit Helena*]

Lysander: She sees not Hermia. Hermia, sleep thou there,
And never mayst thou come Lysander near!
All my powers, address your love and might
To honor Helen, and to be her knight!

[*Exit Lysander*]

Literary terms

"Hermia…Hermia…
Helena…" is an
example of *alliteration*.

Think about it

Do you feel sorry for Helena?

What do you learn about her self-image?

**Act 3
Scene 1**

The tradesmen rehearse their play, sorting out problems as they go through it.

Quince: Here's a marvellous place for our rehearsal. This green plot shall be our stage, this hawthorn **brake** our **tiring-house**; and we will do it in action, as we will do it before the Duke.

thicket
dressing room

Bottom: Peter Quince! There are things in this comedy of Pyramus and Thisbe that will never please. Pyramus must draw a sword to kill himself; which the ladies cannot abide.

Starveling: We must leave the killing out.

Bottom: I have a device to make all well. Write me a prologue to say we will do no harm with our swords, and that Pyramus is not killed indeed. Tell them that I am not Pyramus but Bottom the weaver.

Quince: We will have such a prologue.

Snout: Will not the ladies be afeard of the lion?

Bottom: A lion among ladies is a most dreadful thing.

Snout: Another prologue must tell he is not a lion.

> **Literary terms**
>
> "…ladies…lion…lion… ladies…" is an example of *alliteration*.

Bottom: You must name his name, and half his face must be seen through the lion's neck; he must speak, "Ladies, I am a man" and tell them he is Snug the joiner.

Quince: It shall be so. There is two hard things: to bring the moonlight into a chamber for Pyramus and Thisbe meet by moonlight.

Snout: Doth the moon shine that night we play our play?

Bottom: A calendar!

Quince: Yes, it doth shine that night.

Bottom: Then leave a window, where we play, open; and the moon may shine in.

Quince: Or else one must come in with a bush of thorns and a lantern, and say he comes to present the person of Moonshine. Then we must have a wall for Pyramus and Thisbe did talk through the chink of a wall.

Snout: You can never bring in a wall.

Bottom: Some man must present Wall; and let him have some plaster to signify wall. Let him hold his fingers thus, and through that cranny shall Pyramus and Thisbe whisper.

Quince: Then all is well. Rehearse your parts. Pyramus, You begin: when you have spoken your speech, enter in to that brake; and so every one according to his cue.

Think about it

Do the tradesmen think their audience can tell the difference between reality and a staged play?

What might Shakespeare be suggesting about dreams and reality?

What have we here? A play?

Thisbe, the flowers of odious savors sweet ...

"Odors, Odors!"

Odors savors sweet.

A stranger Pyramus than e'er played here!

Must I speak now?

Ay.

Most radiant Pyramus: most lily-white of hue, of color like the red rose on triumphant briar; I'll meet thee, Pyramus, at Ninny's tomb.

"Ninus' tomb," man! You must not speak that yet. You speak all your part at once, cues and all.

Puck uses his magic to put an ass's head on Bottom. Titania wakes and falls in love with him!

Pyramus, enter! Your cue is past.

If I were fair, Thisbe, I were only thine.

O monstrous! Help!

Why do they run away?

What do I see on thee?

Thou art translated.

This is to make an ass of me, to fright me. I will sing, that they shall hear I am not afraid.

Thou art translated – You've changed

Mine ear . . . thy note – I love the sound of your voice
So is . . . thy shape – And the way you look

You should have little reason for that. Yet reason and love keep little company together nowadays.

Thou art as wise as thou art beautiful.

Thou shalt remain here, whether thou wilt or no. I'll give thee fairies to attend on thee.

Be kind and courteous to this gentleman.

Lead him to my bower. Tie up my lover's tongue, bring him silently.

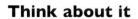

Think about it

How does Titania sound threatening?

| Act 3 Scene 2 | Puck tells Oberon what he has done and what has happened to Titania. Oberon realizes Puck has made a mistake with Lysander. He orders him to fetch Helena while he charms Demetrius' eyes. |

I wonder if Titania be awaked.

How now, mad spirit?

My mistress with a monster is in love.

*A crew of **rude mechanicals**
Were met together to rehearse a play.
The shallowest thick-skin
Who Pyramus presented, entered a brake.
When I did see him at this advantage take,
An ass's **nole** I fixèd on his head.
When they him spy, away his fellows fly.
In that moment, Titania waked,
And straightaway loved an ass.*

*This falls out better than I could devise. But hast thou yet **latched** the Athenian's eyes with love juice, as I bid thee do?*

*I took him sleeping and the Athenian woman by his side that when he waked **of force** she must be eyed.*

rude mechanicals – simple workmen
nole – head

latched – moistened
of force – of necessity; inevitably

What hast thou done? Thou hast mistaken quite.

About the wood go swifter than the wind, and Helena of Athens find.

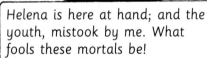

See thou bring her here.

I'll charm his eyes against she do appear.

Helena is here at hand; and the youth, mistook by me. What fools these mortals be!

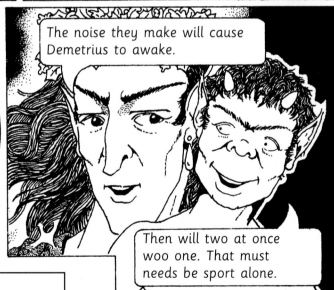

The noise they make will cause Demetrius to awake.

Then will two at once woo one. That must needs be sport alone.

Think about it

What is Puck's attitude to his mistake?

About the wood go – Go through the forest

With both Lysander and Demetrius in love with Helena, she thinks they are making fun of her. Hermia cannot believe what is happening!

Lysander: Why should you think that I woo in scorn?
Look when I vow, I weep.
How can these things in me seem scorn to you
Bearing the badge of faith to prove them true?

Helena: You do advance your cunning more and more.
These vows are Hermia's: will you **give her o'er**?

abandon her

Lysander: I had no judgment when to her I swore.

Helena: Nor none, in my mind, now you give her o'er.

Lysander: Demetrius loves her, and he loves not you.

Demetrius: [*Waking*] O Helen,
To what, my love, shall I compare thine **eyne**?
Crystal is muddy. O how ripe in show
Thy lips, those kissing cherries, tempting grow!
O let me kiss
This princess of pure white, this seal of bliss!

eyes

> **Literary terms**
>
> "Crystal is muddy" is an example of an *oxymoron*.

Helena: O spite! O hell! I see you all are bent
To set against me for your merriment.
If you were civil, and knew courtesy,
You would not do me thus much injury.
Can you not hate me, as I know you do,
But you must join in souls to mock me too?
If you were men, as men you are in show,
You would not use a gentle lady so.
You both are rivals, and love Hermia:
And now both rivals to mock Helena.

Lysander: You are unkind, Demetrius,
For you love Hermia; this you know I know;
And here, with all good will, with all my heart,
In Hermia's love I yield you up my part;
And yours of Helena to me bequeath
Whom I do love, and will do till my death.

You can have Hermia and give me Helena

Helena: Never did mockers waste more idle breath.

Demetrius: Lysander, keep thy Hermia; I will none.
If e'er I loved her, all that love is gone.
My heart to her but as guest-wise sojourned,
And now to Helen is it home returned,
There to remain.

I only loved her for a short while and now my love …

Lysander: Helen, it is not so.

Demetrius: Look where thy love comes: yonder is
thy dear.   [*Enter Hermia*]

Hermia: Thou art not by mine eye, Lysander, found;
Mine ear, I thank it, brought me to thy sound.
But why unkindly didst thou leave me so?

Lysander: Why should he stay whom love doth press to go?

Hermia: What love could press Lysander from my side?

Lysander: Lysander's love would not let him bide.
Fair Helena!
Why seek'st thou me? Could not this make thee know
The hate I bare thee made me leave thee so?

Literary terms

"Lysander's love would not let…" is an example of *alliteration*.

Hermia: You speak not as you think. It cannot be!

Helena: She is one of this confederacy!
They have conjoined all three
To fashion this false sport **in spite of** me.

She's in this with them!

to spite

Hermia! Ungrateful maid!

Is all we two have shared forgot? Schooldays' friendship, childhood innocence?

Will you join with men in scorning your poor friend?

I scorn you not. It seems that you scorn me.

Have you not set Lysander to follow me, and made your other love, Demetrius, to call me goddess?

I understand not what you mean by this.

When I turn my back, wink at each other. Fare well.

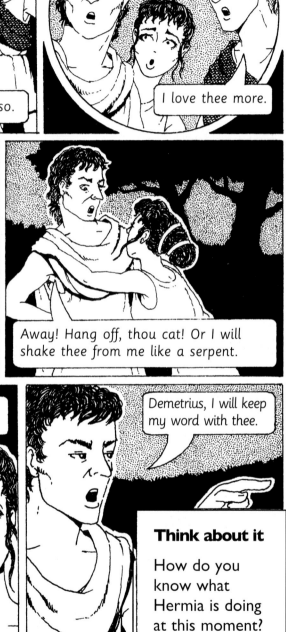

Think about it

How do you know what Hermia is doing at this moment?

A weak bond holds you; I'll not trust your word.

Should I hurt her? Although I hate her, I'll not harm her.

Can you do me greater harm than hate?

I do hate thee, and love Helena.

You thief of love! Have you come by night and stol'n my love's heart?

Fine! Will you tear impatient answers from my gentle tongue? You puppet you!

"Puppet?"

She hath made compare between our statures.

Are you grown so high in his esteem because I am so dwarfish and so low?

Thou painted maypole!

Let her not hurt me. You may think because she is lower than myself, that I can match her.

"Lower?"

Do not be so bitter with me. I never wronged you, save that, in love unto Demetrius, I told him of your stealth into this wood.

To Athens will I, and follow you no further. Let me go.

Get you gone! Who is't that hinders you?

A foolish heart that I leave behind.

With Lysander?

With Demetrius.

Be not afraid; she shall not harm thee, Helena.

No, she shall not.

Think about it

How does the dialogue itself give stage directions?

Oberon: **This is thy negligence: still thou mistak'st**,
Or else committ'st thy knaveries wilfully.

This is your carelessness: you've either made a mistake or done this deliberately.

Puck: Believe me, king of shadows, I mistook.
Did not you tell me I should know the man
By the Athenian garments he had on?
And **so far blameless proves my enterprise**
That I have 'nointed an Athenian's eyes:
And so far am I glad it did so sort,
As this their jangling I esteem a sport.

Literary terms

"king of shadows" is an example of a *metaphor*.

I'm not guilty

I think their argument is good fun.

Oberon: These lovers seek a place to fight.
Robin, overcast the night;
Lead these rivals so astray
As one come not within another's way.
Like to Lysander sometime frame thy tongue,
And some time rail thou like Demetrius,
Till o'er their brows sleep
With leaden legs and **batty** wings doth creep.
Then crush this **herb** into Lysander's eye,
Whose liquor hath to take from thence all error.
When they next wake all shall seem a dream
And back to Athens shall the lovers wend.
I'll to my queen, and beg her Indian boy;
And then I will her **charmèd** eye release
From monster's view, and all things shall be peace.

Sometimes try to sound like Lysander, and at other times like Demetrius

batlike
plant, flower

bewitched

Puck: My fairy lord, this must be done with haste,
For night's swift dragons cut the clouds full fast;
And yonder shines **Aurora's harbinger**,
At whose approach, ghosts wand'ring here and there
Troop home to churchyards.
Spirits already to their wormy beds are gone.

Dawn's messenger – the first light of morning

38

Oberon: But we are spirits of another sort;
I with the Morning's love have oft made sport.
But make no delay;
We may effect this business yet ere day.   [*Exit*]

Puck: Up and down, up and down,
I will lead them up and down.

Think about it

What evidence is there that Oberon has good intentions?

Puck prevents Demetrius and Lysander from meeting. The four lovers are tired. They fall asleep in the fog, without seeing each other.

Here comes one.

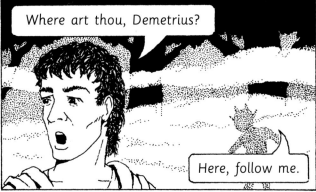

Where art thou, Demetrius?

Here, follow me.

Lysander, where dost thou hide?

Follow my voice.

When I come where he calls, he is gone. I followed fast; but faster did he fly.

Here will rest me. Come gentle day, I'll find Demetrius.

Coward, why com'st thou not?

Thou runn'st and dar'st not stand. Thou mock'st me.

Faintness constraineth me to measure out my length on this cold bed. By day's approach look to be visited.

O weary night. **Sleep, steal me awhile from mine own company.**

Yet but three? Come one more.

I can no further crawl. Here will I rest me till the break of day.

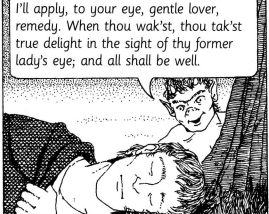

I'll apply, to your eye, gentle lover, remedy. When thou wak'st, thou tak'st true delight in the sight of thy former lady's eye; and all shall be well.

Faintness ... cold bed – I'm so tired that I'm going to have to lie down
Sleep ... company – Let me sleep and forget my worries

Literary terms

"Sleep, steal me" is an example of *personification*.

Titania is released from the spell. Puck takes off Bottom's ass's head. Order is about to be restored.

Come sit down, while I kiss thy fair large ears.

Scratch my head.

I must to the barber's, for methinks I am marvellous hairy about the face.

Wilt thou hear some music, my sweet love?

Or say, sweet love, what thou desirest to eat?

I have a great desire to a **bottle of hay**.

Sleep, and I will wind thee in my arms. O how I love thee!

bottle of hay – bundle of hay

Now I do begin to pity; for, meeting her of late behind the wood I taunted her. She begged my patience. I did ask of her her changeling child which straight she gave me. Now I have the boy, I will undo her eyes.

Puck, take this from off the head of this Athenian. May all to Athens back again repair, and think no more of this night's accidents but as a dream.

First I will release the fairy queen.

What visions have I seen! Methought I was enamoured of an ass.

There lies your love.

in amity – friends again

Act 4 Scene 1	The lovers are woken up. Because Demetrius now loves Helena, Theseus tells Egeus that the couples will marry. They all return to Athens.

Theseus: My love shall hear the music of my hounds.
Let them go. But what are these?

Egeus: My lord, this is my daughter here asleep,
And this Lysander; this Demetrius is, this Helena.
I wonder of their being here together.

Theseus: No doubt they rose up early, to **observe**
The rite of May.
Egeus, is not this the day
That Hermia should give answer of her choice?

celebrate May Day

Egeus: It is, my lord.

Theseus: Go, bid the huntsmen wake them with their horns.
                         [*The lovers are woken up*]
Good morrow friends. Saint Valentine is past.
I pray you all, stand up.
I know you two are rival enemies;
How comes this gentle concord in the world,
That hatred is so far from jealousy
To sleep by hate, and fear no emnity?

So why are you here together – and in peace?

Lysander: My lord, I cannot truly say how I came here.
I think I came with Hermia hither; our intent
Was to be gone from Athens, where we might,
Without the peril of the Athenian law . . .

Egeus: Enough! I beg the law upon his head!
They would have stol'n away, they would, Demetrius,
Thereby to have defeated you and me:
You of your wife, and me of my consent,
Of my consent that she should be your wife.

Demetrius: Fair Helen told me of their stealth,
And I in fury hither followed them,
Fair Helena in fancy following me.
I **wot** not by what power   know
But my love to Hermia melted as the snow.
The object and the pleasure of mine eye
Is only Helena. To her, my lord,
Was I bethroth'd ere I saw Hermia.

Theseus: Egeus, I will overbear your will;
In the temple, with us,
These couples shall eternally be **knit**.   married
Away with us to Athens;
We'll hold a feast in great solemnity.
        [*Exit Theseus, Hippolyta, Egeus and hunters*]

Demetrius: These things seem like far-off mountains
Turnèd into clouds.

Hermia: Methinks I see these things with parted eye,   It's as if everything is blurred.
When everything seems double.

Helena: So methinks;
And I have found Demetrius like a jewel,
Mine own, and not mine own.

Demetrius: Are you sure that we are awake? It seems to me
That yet we sleep, we dream. Do you not think
The Duke was here, and bid us follow him?

Hermia: Yea, and my father.

Helena: And Hippolyta.

Lysander: And he did bid us follow to the temple.

Demetrius: Why then, we are awake: let's follow him,
And by the way let us recount our dreams.
                                 [*They leave*]

Literary terms

"Fair… fury… followed…
fair… fancy following…"
is an example of *alliteration*.

Think about it

How must Egeus be
feeling now?

What is Shakespeare
trying to tell us
about love?

 When my cue comes, call me.

 Left me asleep!

 I have had a dream. Methought I was ... I will get Peter Quince to write a ballad of this dream: it shall be called "Bottom's Dream" and I will sing it in the latter end of a play before the Duke.

| **Act 4 Scene 2** | Bottom returns to Athens – much to the relief of Quince and the others! |

 Have you sent to Bottom's house? Is he come home yet?

He cannot be heard of.

If he come not, the play is **marred**.

 You have not a man in all Athens able to **discharge** Pyramus but he.

 The Duke is coming from the temple, and there is two or three lords and ladies more married. If our sport had gone forward, we had all been made men.

 Where are these lads?

Bottom!

I will tell you everything.

Let us hear.

All that I will tell you is, the Duke hath dined. Get your **apparel** together; meet at the palace. Our play is preferred. Eat no onions, nor garlic. Away!

marred – ruined
discharge – play
apparel – stuff

47

<table>
<tr><td>**Act 5
Scene 1**</td><td>The tradesmen's play, *Pyramus and Thisbe*, is chosen. The wedding party settle down to be entertained.</td></tr>
</table>

'Tis strange that these lovers speak of.

More strange than true. Lovers and madmen have such seething brains. The lunatic, the lover, and the poet are **of imagination all compact**.

But all the story of the night told over, **grows to something of great constancy**.

Here come the lovers. What shall we have to wear away three hours between our supper and bedtime?

Philostrate. What have you for this evening?

Make choice, your Highness.

"A tedious brief scene of young Pyramus and his love Thisbe, very tragical mirth"? "Merry" and "tragical"? "Tedious" and "brief"? What are they that do play it?

Men that work in Athens here.

We will hear it.

No, my noble lord, it is not for you. I have heard it and it is nothing.

Go bring them in; and take your places, ladies.

of imagintion all compact – full of fantasies
grows to ... constancy – seems as if they are telling the truth

Literary terms

"tragical mirth" is an example of an *oxymoron*.

48

If we offend, it is with our goodwill. That you should think, we come not to offend, but with goodwill.

He knows not **the stop**.

Gentles, this man is Pyramus; this beauteous lady, Thisbe.

This man, "Wall"; and through Wall's chink, they are content to whisper.

This man, with lantern, dog, and bush of thorn, Moonshine.

These lovers think to meet at Ninus' tomb. Lion, the trusty Thisbe did scare away. As she fled, her **mantle** she did fall, which Lion with bloody mouth did stain.

Anon comes Pyramus and finds Thisbe's mantle slain; whereat, with blade he bravely **broached** his boiling bloody breast.

Thisbe his dagger drew, and died.

the stop – how to use the full stop
mantle – scarf
broached – stabbed

Literary terms

"with blade he bravely broached his boiling bloody breast" is an example of *alliteration*.

I, one Snout by name, present a wall.

Pyramus draws near the wall; silence!

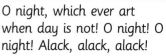

O night, which ever art when day is not! O night! O night! Alack, alack, alack!

O wall, O sweet, O lovely wall, show me thy chink.

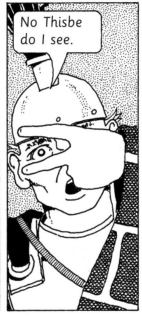

No Thisbe do I see.

O wicked wall, cursed be thy stones for thus deceiving me!

The wall should curse again.

No sir, he should not. "Deceiving me" is Thisbe's cue: she is to enter now, and I am to spy her through the wall.

Think about it

Where does Bottom come out of role?

What does he fail to understand?

50

Ladies, you may quake and tremble here. Then, know that I, as Snug the joiner, am a lion.

A very gentle beast.

This lantern doth the hornèd moon present; myself the Man i' th' Moon do seem to be.

The man should be put into the lantern. How is it else the Man i' th' Moon?

He dares not come there for the candle.

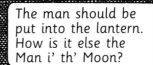

I am aweary of this moon.

All I have to say is; I the Man i' th' Moon; this thornbush my thornbush; and this dog my dog.

Here comes Thisbe.

This is old Ninny's tomb. Where is my love?

Well roared, Lion!

Well run, Thisbe!

Well shone, Moon!

And then came Pyramus.

Sweet Moon, I thank thee for thy sunny beams.

Eyes, do you see? What! Stained with blood?

Out sword, and wound Pyramus.

Thus die I, thus, thus, thus!

Now am I dead. Now die, die, die, die, die.

With the help of a surgeon he might yet recover, and prove an ass.

How chance Moonshine is gone, before Thisbe comes back and finds her lover?

She will find him by starlight. Here she comes, and her passion ends the play.

Methinks she should not use a long one for such a Pyramus; I hope she will be brief.

No, I assure you, the wall is down that parted their fathers.

Will it please you to see the **epilogue**, or a **Bergomask** dance?

No epilogue; your play needs no excuse. But come, your Bergomask.

The **iron tongue of midnight** hath told twelve. Lovers, to bed! 'Tis almost fairy time.

epilogue – short poem or speech to end the play
Bergomask – an Italian folk dance
iron tongue of midnight – the midnight bell (with its iron clapper)

We ... frolic – We can play and enjoy ourselves

<table>
<tr><td>

**Act 5
Scene 1**

</td><td>

Puck appeals to the audience. He tells them if they didn't like the play, then they must imagine they dreamed it and the actors will do better in the future.

</td></tr>
</table>

If we shadows have offended,
Think but this and all is mended,
That you have but **slumbered** here
While these visions did appear.
And this weak and idle theme,
No more yielding but a dream.
Gentles, do not reprehend:
If you pardon, we will **mend**.
And, as I am an honest Puck,
If we have unearnèd luck
Now to 'scape the **serpent's tongue**,
We will **make amends ere long**;
Else the Puck a liar call.
So, goodnight unto you all.
Give me your hands, if we be friends,
And Robin shall restore amends.

THE END

slumbered – slept
mend – do better in future
serpent's tongue – hisses

make amends ere long – soon make it up to you
Give me your hands – Applaud